How To Be A Serial Killer (Novelty Book)

This book is sold as a novelty item only.

A novinka publication.
Novinka: Czech for novelty.

Copyright © 2018 by Steven David Lampley

All rights reserved. This book or any portion thereof may not be reproduced or used in any manner whatsoever the express written permission of the author except for the use of brief quotations in a book review.

Printed in the United States of America

Oliphant Publishing

First Printing, 2018

ISBN-13: 9781730768750

This book is sold as a novelty item only.

1. never let them know your next move.

This book is sold as a novelty item only.

This book is sold as a novelty item only.

This book is sold as a novelty item only.

This book is sold as a novelty item only.

This book is sold as a novelty item only.

This book is sold as a novelty item only.

This book is sold as a novelty item only.

This book is sold as a novelty item only.

This book is sold as a novelty item only.

This book is sold as a novelty item only.

This book is sold as a novelty item only.

This book is sold as a novelty item only.

This book is sold as a novelty item only.

This book is sold as a novelty item only.

This book is sold as a novelty item only.

This book is sold as a novelty item only.

This book is sold as a novelty item only.

This book is sold as a novelty item only.

This book is sold as a novelty item only.

This book is sold as a novelty item only.

This book is sold as a novelty item only.

This book is sold as a novelty item only.

This book is sold as a novelty item only.

This book is sold as a novelty item only.

This book is sold as a novelty item only.

This book is sold as a novelty item only.

This book is sold as a novelty item only.

This book is sold as a novelty item only.

This book is sold as a novelty item only.

This book is sold as a novelty item only.

This book is sold as a novelty item only.

This book is sold as a novelty item only.

This book is sold as a novelty item only.

This book is sold as a novelty item only.

This book is sold as a novelty item only.

This book is sold as a novelty item only.

This book is sold as a novelty item only.

This book is sold as a novelty item only.

This book is sold as a novelty item only.

This book is sold as a novelty item only.

This book is sold as a novelty item only.

This book is sold as a novelty item only.

This book is sold as a novelty item only.

This book is sold as a novelty item only.

This book is sold as a novelty item only.

This book is sold as a novelty item only.

This book is sold as a novelty item only.

This book is sold as a novelty item only.

This book is sold as a novelty item only.

This book is sold as a novelty item only.

This book is sold as a novelty item only.

This book is sold as a novelty item only.

This book is sold as a novelty item only.

This book is sold as a novelty item only.

This book is sold as a novelty item only.

This book is sold as a novelty item only.

This book is sold as a novelty item only.

This book is sold as a novelty item only.

This book is sold as a novelty item only.

This book is sold as a novelty item only.

This book is sold as a novelty item only.

This book is sold as a novelty item only.

This book is sold as a novelty item only.

This book is sold as a novelty item only.

This book is sold as a novelty item only.

This book is sold as a novelty item only.

This book is sold as a novelty item only.

This book is sold as a novelty item only.

This book is sold as a novelty item only.

This book is sold as a novelty item only.

This book is sold as a novelty item only.

This book is sold as a novelty item only.

This book is sold as a novelty item only.

This book is sold as a novelty item only.

This book is sold as a novelty item only.

This book is sold as a novelty item only.

This book is sold as a novelty item only.

This book is sold as a novelty item only.

This book is sold as a novelty item only.

This book is sold as a novelty item only.

This book is sold as a novelty item only.

This book is sold as a novelty item only.

This book is sold as a novelty item only.

This book is sold as a novelty item only.

This book is sold as a novelty item only.

This book is sold as a novelty item only.

This book is sold as a novelty item only.

This book is sold as a novelty item only.

This book is sold as a novelty item only.

This book is sold as a novelty item only.

This book is sold as a novelty item only.

This book is sold as a novelty item only.

This book is sold as a novelty item only.

This book is sold as a novelty item only.

This book is sold as a novelty item only.

This book is sold as a novelty item only.

This book is sold as a novelty item only.

This book is sold as a novelty item only.

This book is sold as a novelty item only.

This book is sold as a novelty item only.

This book is sold as a novelty item only.

This book is sold as a novelty item only.

This book is sold as a novelty item only.

This book is sold as a novelty item only.

This book is sold as a novelty item only.

This book is sold as a novelty item only.

This book is sold as a novelty item only.

This book is sold as a novelty item only.

This book is sold as a novelty item only.

This book is sold as a novelty item only.

This book is sold as a novelty item only.

This book is sold as a novelty item only.

This book is sold as a novelty item only.

This book is sold as a novelty item only.

This book is sold as a novelty item only.

This book is sold as a novelty item only.

This book is sold as a novelty item only.

This book is sold as a novelty item only.

This book is sold as a novelty item only.

This book is sold as a novelty item only.

This book is sold as a novelty item only.

This book is sold as a novelty item only.

This book is sold as a novelty item only.

This book is sold as a novelty item only.

This book is sold as a novelty item only.

This book is sold as a novelty item only.

This book is sold as a novelty item only.

This book is sold as a novelty item only.

This book is sold as a novelty item only.

This book is sold as a novelty item only.

This book is sold as a novelty item only.

This book is sold as a novelty item only.

This book is sold as a novelty item only.

This book is sold as a novelty item only.

This book is sold as a novelty item only.

This book is sold as a novelty item only.

This book is sold as a novelty item only.

This book is sold as a novelty item only.

This book is sold as a novelty item only.

This book is sold as a novelty item only.

This book is sold as a novelty item only.

This book is sold as a novelty item only.

This book is sold as a novelty item only.

This book is sold as a novelty item only.

This book is sold as a novelty item only.

This book is sold as a novelty item only.

This book is sold as a novelty item only.

This book is sold as a novelty item only.

This book is sold as a novelty item only.

This book is sold as a novelty item only.

This book is sold as a novelty item only.

This book is sold as a novelty item only.

This book is sold as a novelty item only.

This book is sold as a novelty item only.

This book is sold as a novelty item only.

This book is sold as a novelty item only.

This book is sold as a novelty item only.

This book is sold as a novelty item only.

This book is sold as a novelty item only.

This book is sold as a novelty item only.

This book is sold as a novelty item only.

This book is sold as a novelty item only.

This book is sold as a novelty item only.

This book is sold as a novelty item only.

This book is sold as a novelty item only.

This book is sold as a novelty item only.

This book is sold as a novelty item only.

This book is sold as a novelty item only.

This book is sold as a novelty item only.

This book is sold as a novelty item only.

This book is sold as a novelty item only.

This book is sold as a novelty item only.

This book is sold as a novelty item only.

This book is sold as a novelty item only.

This book is sold as a novelty item only.

This book is sold as a novelty item only.

This book is sold as a novelty item only.

This book is sold as a novelty item only.

This book is sold as a novelty item only.

This book is sold as a novelty item only.

This book is sold as a novelty item only.

This book is sold as a novelty item only.

This book is sold as a novelty item only.

This book is sold as a novelty item only.

This book is sold as a novelty item only.

This book is sold as a novelty item only.

This book is sold as a novelty item only.

This book is sold as a novelty item only.

This book is sold as a novelty item only.

This book is sold as a novelty item only.

This book is sold as a novelty item only.

This book is sold as a novelty item only.

This book is sold as a novelty item only.

This book is sold as a novelty item only.

This book is sold as a novelty item only.

This book is sold as a novelty item only.

This book is sold as a novelty item only.

This book is sold as a novelty item only.

This book is sold as a novelty item only.

This book is sold as a novelty item only.

This book is sold as a novelty item only.

This book is sold as a novelty item only.

This book is sold as a novelty item only.

This book is sold as a novelty item only.

This book is sold as a novelty item only.

This book is sold as a novelty item only.

This book is sold as a novelty item only.

This book is sold as a novelty item only.

This book is sold as a novelty item only.

This book is sold as a novelty item only.

This book is sold as a novelty item only.

This book is sold as a novelty item only.

Printed in Great Britain
by Amazon